Sketching Scripture

Small Group Devotionals
&
Bible Illustrating Templates

Devotionals by Lauren Reeves

Illustrations by April Roycroft

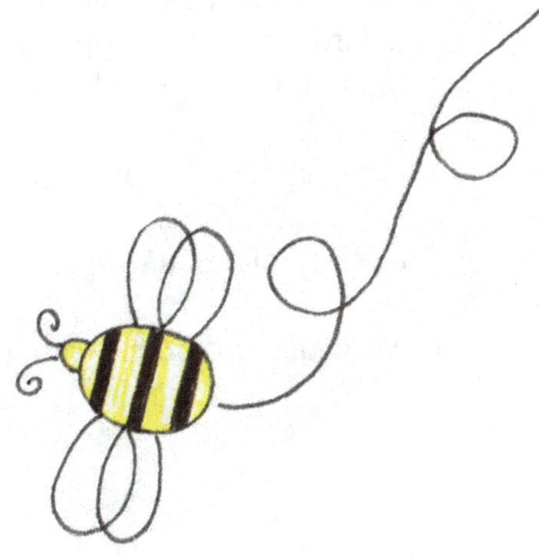

Contents

Small Group Instructions

We are so excited you've chosen to lead a Bible illustration small group! We couldn't be happier about offering a creative way to get together with friends and grow closer to the Lord through art, God's Word, and deep discussion-driven fellowship.

This book not only includes original artwork to guide you in illustrating your Bibles, but it also includes coordinating devotionals to help you and your group dig deeper in scripture together with the Lord.

Each member should purchase a Sketching Scripture book so they can read the devotionals before class and have their own templates to use in class. Participants should read the short devotional each week before they come and should be encouraged to complete the discussion questions before they come to class as well. Allowing group members to share their answers to these questions will help drive the discussion deeper as everyone works on their Bible illustrations. We believe that participating in art with other people can be therapeutic and can aide in cultivating a relaxed, low-pressure environment where people may be more likely to authentically share and get to know one another.

Every so often we encounter people who refuse to color in their bible, and that's ok! Suggest that they bring a journal to color inside of instead.

If you'd like, you can introduce new art media each week. Attendance will be more successful if members understand they will be able to participate in different forms of bible illustrating each week. Visit our website at www.sketchingscripture.com. We have posted answers to some frequently asked questions as well as Bible illustrating videos with tips and tricks.

As a convenience for your members (and to deter multiple questions beforehand), we recommend that leaders provide most of the supplies for everyone to share each week. Below is a list of those recommended art media supplies. Also included below is a list of items that each individual participant should purchase and bring with them.

A minimum of two hours is necessary for meetings. Two hours should be just enough time to briefly explain the new media for the week and for everyone to complete their illustrations while having conversations pertaining to the discussion questions. Feel free to build upon the previous week's instruction, mixing medias and techniques as you go.

Thank you for joining us in this unique small group experience! We are praying earnestly for you!

"Now that you have purified yourselves by obeying the truth so that you have sincere love for each other, love one another deeply, from the heart."
~ 1 Peter 1:22

With Love,
April & Lauren

SUGGESTED SUPPLIES FOR LEADERS TO HAVE AVAILABLE <u>EVERY</u> WEEK:

- Several designs of decorative washi tape to mark completed Bible illustration pages and/or to mark the books of the Bible.
- Paint brushes
- Water cups for rinsing or rewetting paint brushes
- Scissors
- Hair dryer to expedite page drying time
- Foil or paper plates to use to mix paint colors
- Graphite paper for transferring the illustration template onto the Bible page if not free-handing
- Gesso (*This is a painting-surface primer that can be lightly applied to Bible pages to avoid bleed-through using old gift cards or wide popsicle sticks. If Gesso is used, a hairdryer can be used to speed dry time.) **Optional***
- Old gift cards or wide popsicle sticks to apply Gesso

SUPPLIES TO BE ADDED BY LEADER OVER TIME (depending on budget, pick a few that are affordable or purchase all to be <u>shared</u> by the class):

Week One Art Media
Crayola® Twistable Pencils or any kind of map colors

Week Two Art Media
Watercolors (with or without Gesso)

Week Three Art Media
Gelatos* (with or without Gesso)
**Gelatos are pigment sticks that have a creamy consistency and can be blended with or without water.*

Week Four Art Media
Various colors of acrylic paint (with or without Gesso)

Week Five Art Media
White Uni-ball Signo® Gel Pen for adding white back to colored areas and Prismacolor® Premier Double-Ended Brush Tip Markers for adding shadows to lettering or images (we recommend Cool Grey 40% and Cool Grey 60% for shadowing)

Week Six Art Media
Neocolor II Water-Soluble Crayons

SUPPLIES FOR PARTICIPANTS TO BRING EACH WEEK:

- Journaling Bible or a Bible-sized journal
- Mechanical pencil (This is used to draw/trace the template from the workbook.)
- Black micron pens - various sizes preferred (These are used to outline the illustrations each week before or after coloring.)

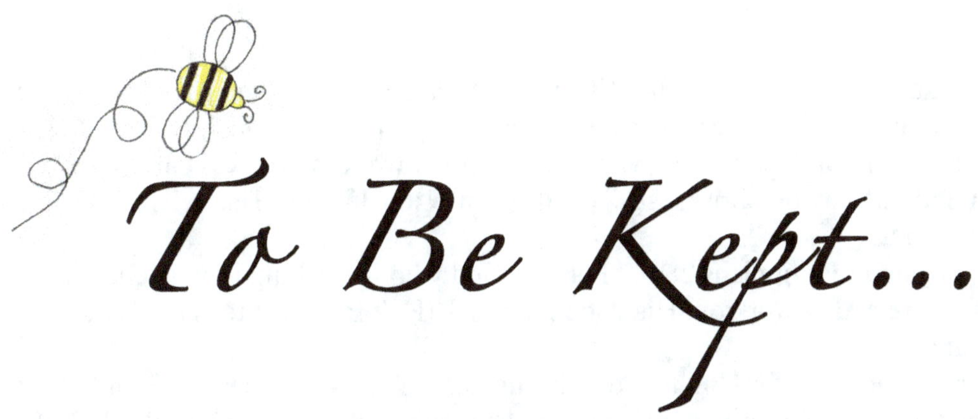

To Be Kept...

by Lauren Reeves

I'm convinced there's a longing in every woman to be fully known; a longing for those close to her to know the desirable along with the undesirable and yet love her and want to keep her still.

The problem is many of us somehow formed the belief that the only way we can be loved is if we are perfect, desirable, or right.... all the time. It can be exhausting.

In our intense pursuit of perfection to secure the love of others (and probably God's love as well), our authenticity wanes. The character we play begins to take the stage as we hide this thought or that thought, as we cover up or justify a mistake here or there, or as we give advice, acting as if we've never actually struggled ourselves. This character we play might even portray our bible reading and prayers as being much more regular than they actually are. It's true. I've played this character many times before. But at the very core, the driving force was simply a desire to be loved and kept forever.

One night I was reading Psalm 139. David, divinely inspired by the Holy Spirit, penned some truths in that psalm that began to rip off the mask of perfection that I felt for so long I simply MUST wear.

God is described in this psalm as KNOWING when I sit and when I rise, PERCEIVING my thoughts, and DISCERNING all my ways. It says that before a word is even on my tongue, He knows it completely. And, as if that wasn't enough to prove I can't hide from truly being seen by Him, the psalm says if I make my bed in the depths, He's there. If I rise in the far East or settle in the far West, His right hand holds me fast. If I hide in darkness's covering, even darkness will not be dark to Him. He knows me completely because He created me, knitting me together in my mother's womb.

All those truths spoke to my soul, but here's the verse that did it for me - this is where it clicked: "Your eyes saw my unformed body; all the days ordained for me were written in Your book before one of them came to be" (Psalm 139:16).

Did you get that? All my days, even the imperfect days, were entered into His book BEFORE one of them came to be and BEFORE my body was even formed.

So, if God knew all my failures, all my imperfections, all my deceptions that would be contained in my days here on earth and STILL chose to form me… If He knew all that and STILL chose to draw me to Himself to save me, He really does love me - the real me; the me that can't get it together sometimes; the me that forgets to pray for days and then feels guilt; the me that sometimes says the wrong thing because it feels good; the me that is sometimes "too much" and other times "not enough;" the me that often delights in the praise of man rather than God's approval. Do you see it? He really does love us, y'all – imperfections and everything.

He knew exactly how we would be RIGHT NOW and chose to keep us anyway. We are works in progress, so He sees our potential and the purpose for which He saved us. Paul says, "I am sure of this, that He who started a good work in you will carry it on to completion until the day of Christ Jesus" (Philippians 1:6, HCSB). That tells me He's not giving up on us.

Paul says again in Philippians 2:13, "For it is God who is working in you, enabling you both to desire and to work out His good purpose" (HCSB). That tells me He's partners with us.

No failure is too great for Him to work through. No hurt is too deep for Him to heal. No imperfection is too big for Him to sanctify. But what is the key to all of this? Being honest with Him and others and ourselves. God LOVES authenticity. I can't say it enough. God loves authenticity!

So what do we do? We get authentic. I think Beth Moore says it best in her study on David: "Feelings can be a little like our laundry. Sometimes we can't sort them until we dump them on the table."[1]

So, lay it all out before God and let Him begin to heal your fears, kill your pride, and nurse your exhausted mind back to life. And then, it wouldn't hurt to share with some friends about where you are in your journey. You'll be surprised how vulnerability often breeds an openness and closeness that wasn't there before. Isn't it ironic that we thought that somehow looking like we had it all together would bring us closer to one another? It's just the opposite…with true friends, anyway.

"Therefore, confess your sins to one another and pray for one another, so that you may be healed" (James 5:16, HCSB).

And remember, no matter what you do, what you say, or what you are, you are loved and kept by God.

Discussion Questions

1. Is there a character you play at times in order to appear like you have it all together? If so, what does your character look like?

2. Read Psalm 139:13-16.
    - What was hidden from God?

    - How is God's work described?

    - What does that make you?

---

[1] Taken from *A Heart Like His: Seeking the Heart of God Through a Study of David* by Beth Moore. Copyright © 1996 by LifeWay Press. Reprinted and used by permission.

3. I love projects. Correction… I love to START projects. However, God is not like
    me. What does Philippians 1:6 say? Write it here and emphasize the word
    "completion" artistically somehow.

4. Don't you love, Beth Moore's quote? It said, "Feelings can be a little like our
    laundry. Sometimes we can't sort them until we dump them on the table." What
    do you have going on in your life that you need to "dump on the table?"

5. Read James 5:16. Is there anything we can pray about for you?

*We would love to see your Sketching Scripture art each week. If you post your
completed Bible journaling art on social media, use our hashtag so we can find you!*
#sketchingscripture

Lettering #1

Print

Cursive

- use pencil **FIRST**
- go **SLOW**
- write light
- spellcheck
- go over it with pen
- erase pencil
- do your own version

- fill in lines on the ↓ strokes

ABCDEFGHIJKLMNO
PQRSTUVWXYZ
1234567890
abcdefghijklmnopqr
stuvwxyz !@#*
$ & % ?

Strong and courageous

TRUTH

Jesus

trust & obey ♥ mercies are new

Jesus love

Lord of Lords

in the beginning

Morning Star

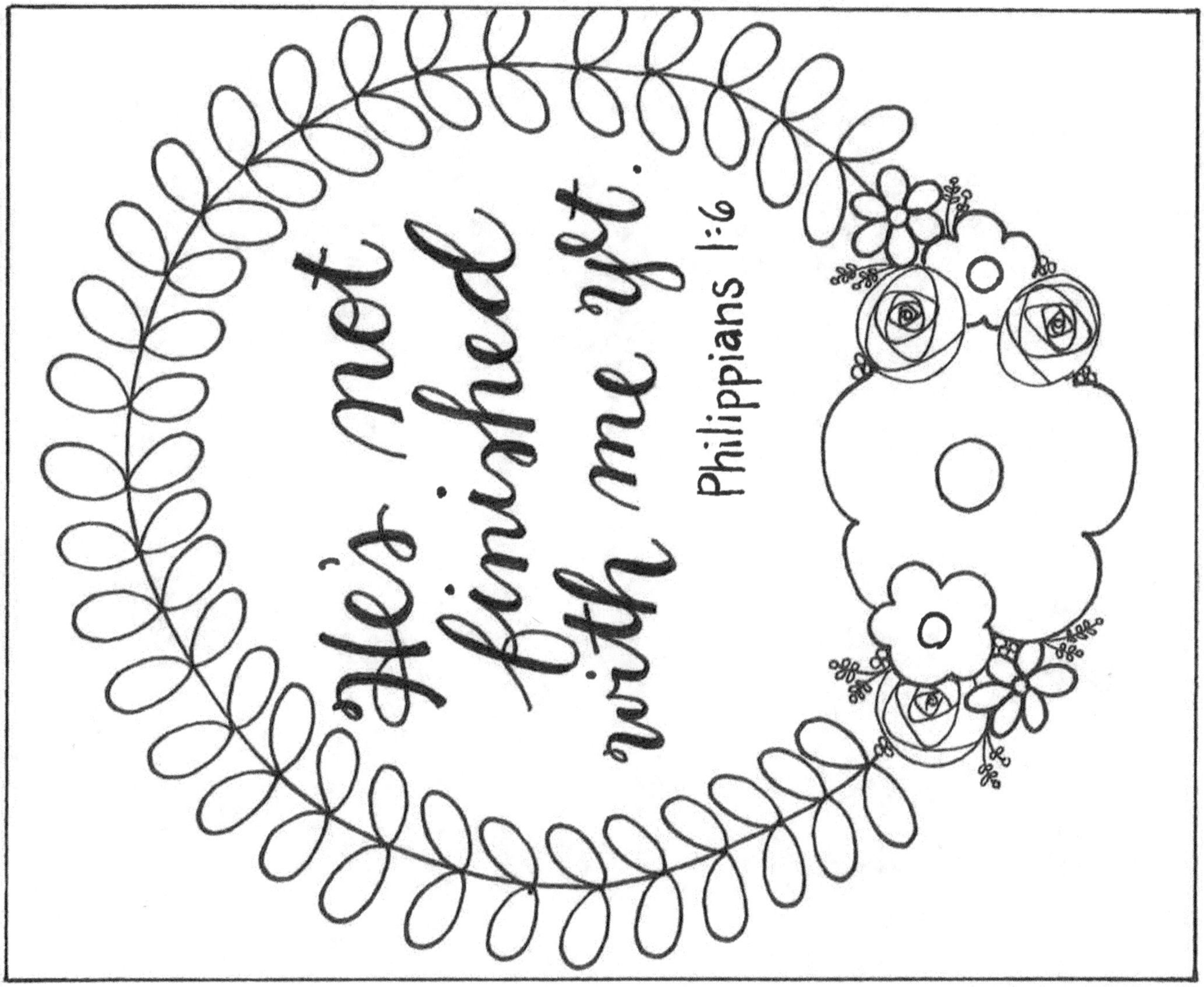

He's not finished with me yet. Philippians 1:6

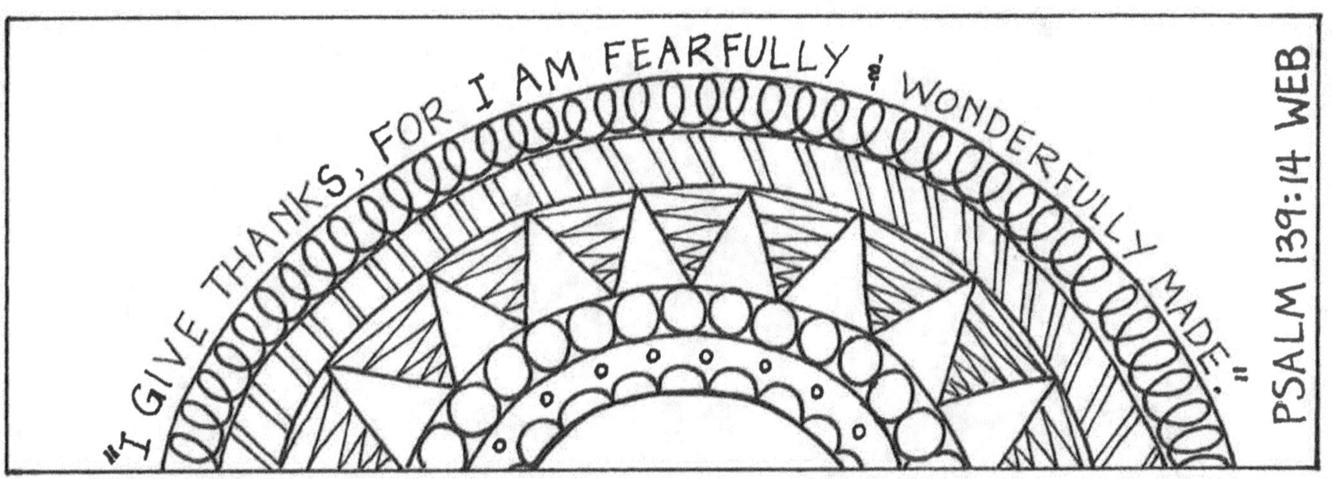

Anti-Venom

by Lauren Reeves

Sometimes I hide. I go to the store and hope I don't see anyone I know. I check out of life with a good book and get aggravated if someone interrupts my escape. I often prefer the company of my horses and dogs to humans (Disclaimer: I am actually very much a people-person contrary to how this is starting out!). I sometimes even get annoyed when people try to call me (or worse yet, come to my door) rather than text me. It's true. These are the ways I hide. Then there are other ways, like when my husband can tell that something is the matter and says, "What's wrong?" And instead of telling him about the battle going on in my mind, I choose to just stand my ground with, "Nothing. I'm fine."

Why do we do this? Sometimes it's just because we're physically tired. But other times I think it's because we are emotionally or spiritually tired and don't want to take the risk of allowing anyone to have the opportunity to hurt us or judge us more, as if we believe we've somehow got it coming to us; as if we are magnets for hurt or judgment if we allow ourselves to walk where people are or let them see into our little world.

Why do we sometimes think this way? And we make this mistake in other ways, too – like believing we aren't beautiful; believing we aren't worthy to be loved; believing if we try something new, we will fail; believing we aren't good enough to be loved or used by God. The list goes on and on. Think of your tendencies. What are you inclined to think about wrongly?

I believe our thinking is the primary struggle in our lives. The secret places of the mind are where the Enemy loves to wreak havoc. Our Enemy LOVES a good secret that he can shame us into believing we can't tell. He loves for us to be isolated. And the more secrets we have and the more we isolate ourselves, naturally, the more alone we feel. Our enemy knows this, so he condemns us and shames us into hiding.

I was jogging the other day with my little English Springer Spaniel. We live on fenced acreage, so Briley runs loose around me as I jog. On this particular day he ran off a little farther than usual and so I called out to him. When he came back to me, I saw something hanging out of his mouth. I told him to drop it, and when he did, I realized it was a freshly shed snakeskin! YUCK!

But as I jogged, I began to think about snakes and how fitting it is that Satan took on that form in the book of Genesis. A snake has no hands or feet - it operates with cunning and craftiness (aka mind games). And when Satan does "bite," his lies are just like venom – working from the inside out. When a snake bites, the venom makes detrimental changes on the inside until eventually (if untreated) it causes paralysis or rotting flesh on the outside.

Isn't that exactly how the enemy works? He tells you false things about who you are and false things about what God and people think about you. And since we only act on what we TRULY believe, if he convinces us we are terrible people, we will act on that belief, hiding ourselves from others out of fear of being known.

The venom is the false beliefs he plants in our heads. And if we don't seek God and His Word, which is the anti-venom, these false beliefs will eventually paralyze us from fulfilling God's purpose for our lives. The Enemy works from the inside out, just like a snake.

If you Google search the differences between guilt and shame and condemnation, you'll find that guilt is feeling sorry for something you've DONE. Shame is feeling sorry for something you ARE. Condemnation is feeling like you've been pronounced to be WRONG AND UNFIT FOR USE.

Of the three, guilt, IF it leads you to godly sorrow and repentance, is the only healthy choice. Shame and condemnation are of the Enemy, and we have to fight against him with Truth and by going to God, our defender, in prayer. God has provided all of the Truth we need to know about who we REALLY are in scripture. Dwell on those things. They are our anti-venom!

Psalm 32 reiterates what we are to do when we are tempted to hide, or isolate ourselves, or keep secrets. David wrote this psalm after committing adultery with Bathsheba and being an accomplice to her husband's murder. Eek! I would DEFINTELY be feeling the need to hide after THAT!! Wouldn't you? But David's response is exactly what makes David "a man after God's own heart." David ran to God EVERY TIME he was in trouble or got himself into trouble.

In Psalm 32:3 he confesses, "When I kept silent, my bones wasted away through my groaning all day long." His secret and his isolation from God were killing him! And it kills us spiritually, too!

In verse 5 he recounts, "Then I acknowledged my sin to You and did not cover up my iniquity. I said, 'I will confess my transgressions to the Lord' – and You forgave the guilt of my sin."

David is so freed and relieved after confessing that he is overjoyed in verse 6 saying, "Therefore let all the faithful pray to You while You may be found; surely the rising of the mighty waters will not reach them. You are my hiding place; You will protect me from trouble and surround me with songs of deliverance."

In verses 8 and 9, God promises those who are willing to come to Him counsel for their heart, protection, instruction, and teaching in the way they should go: "I will instruct and teach you in the way you should go; I will counsel you with My loving eye on you. Do not be like the horse or the mule, which have no understanding but must be controlled by bit and bridle or they will not come to you."

God is saying He doesn't want to have to force us to come to Him when we mess up or are in trouble as you would a horse or mule. He wants us to understand Hebrews 4:16 that says, "Let us then approach God's throne of grace with confidence, so that we may receive mercy and find grace to help us in our time of need."

So if your thoughts are making you feel like you need to run away and hide FROM God rather than run TO God, the Truth, and the Body of Christ, it's a sure sign your mind is being messed with by the Enemy and you need some anti-venom!!

1. What are some ways you hide when you're emotionally or spiritually tired?

2. What lies does the enemy attack your thoughts with most often?

3. Read Ephesians 6:10-11. Whose armor is it? Does this fact encourage independence or dependence?

4. Read Ephesians 6:13-18. Reading about the pieces of armor available to us, how can we use each piece to stand against the Enemy? Pick the one that stands out to you most right now and share your strategy with your group.

5. How might the enemy be paralyzing you from fulfilling God's purpose in your life?

6. Find a scripture that tells you the TRUTH about who you REALLY are. Creatively sketch it below.

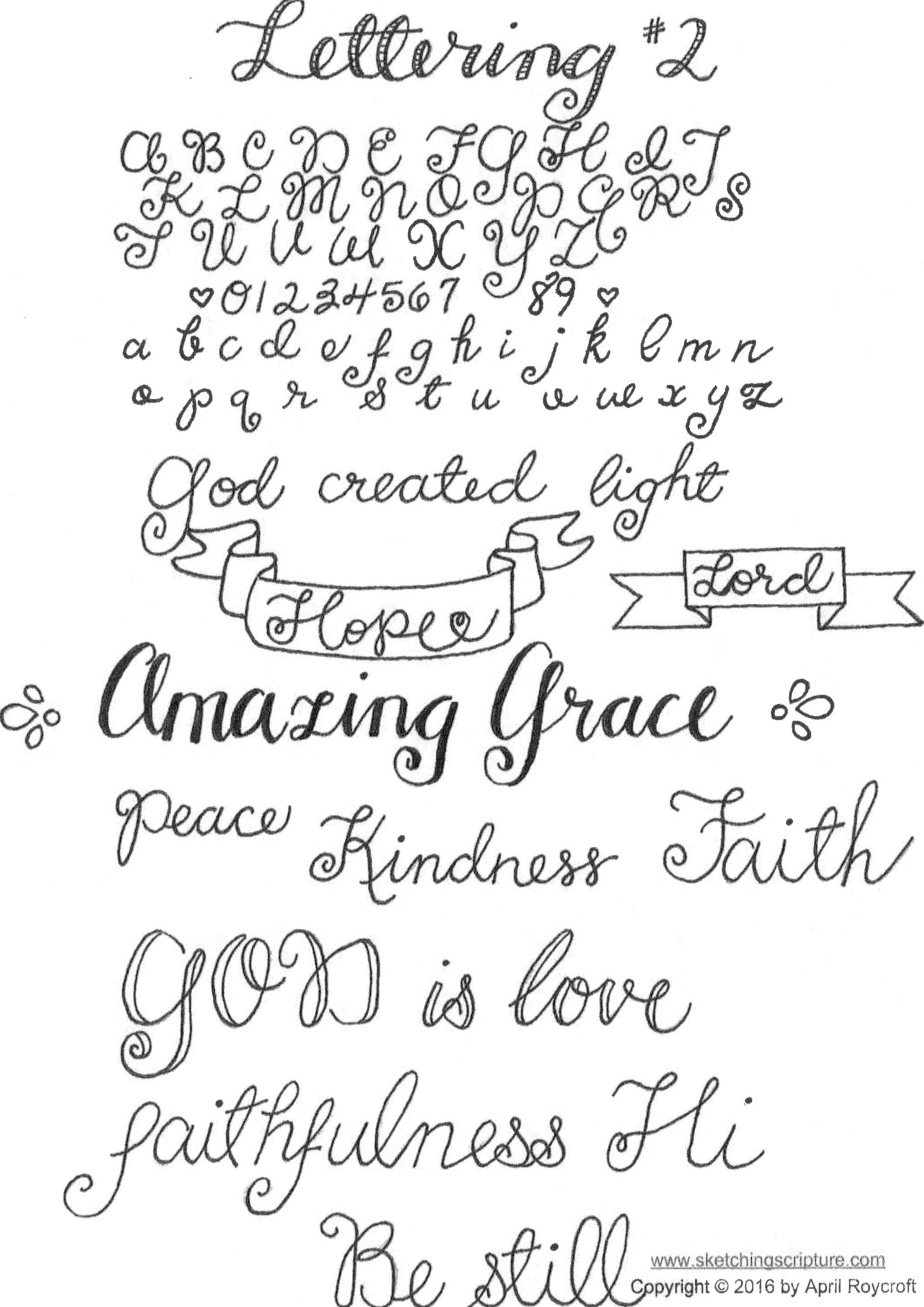

Lettering #2
A B C D E F G H I J
K L M N O P Q R S
T U V U W X Y Z
0 1 2 3 4 5 6 7 8 9
a b c d e f g h i j k l m n
o p q r s t u v w x y z
God created light
Hope
Lord
Amazing Grace
Peace Kindness Faith
GOD is love
faithfulness Hi
Be still

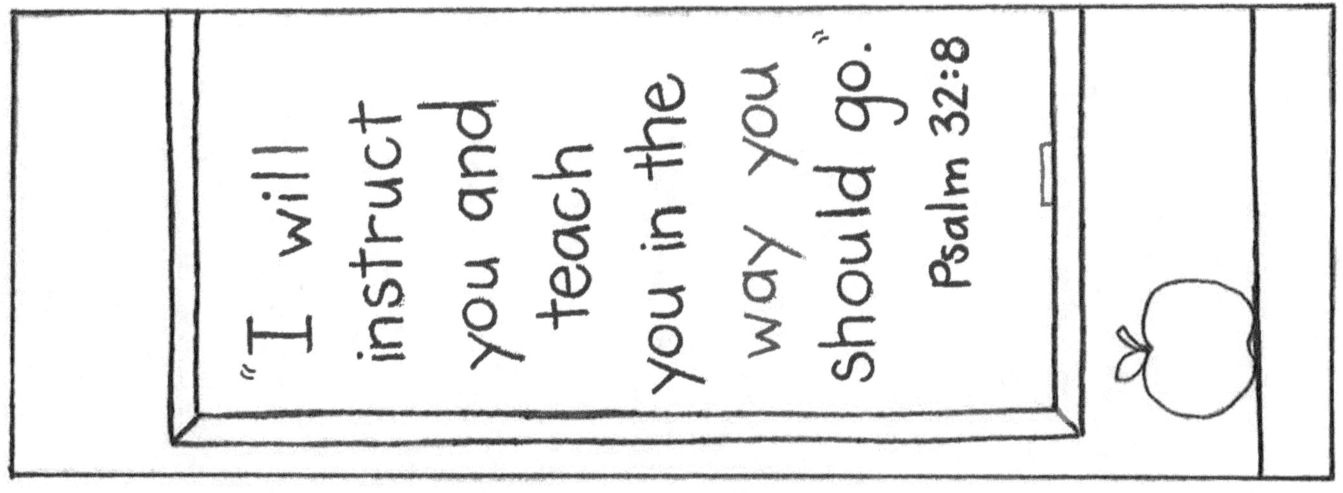

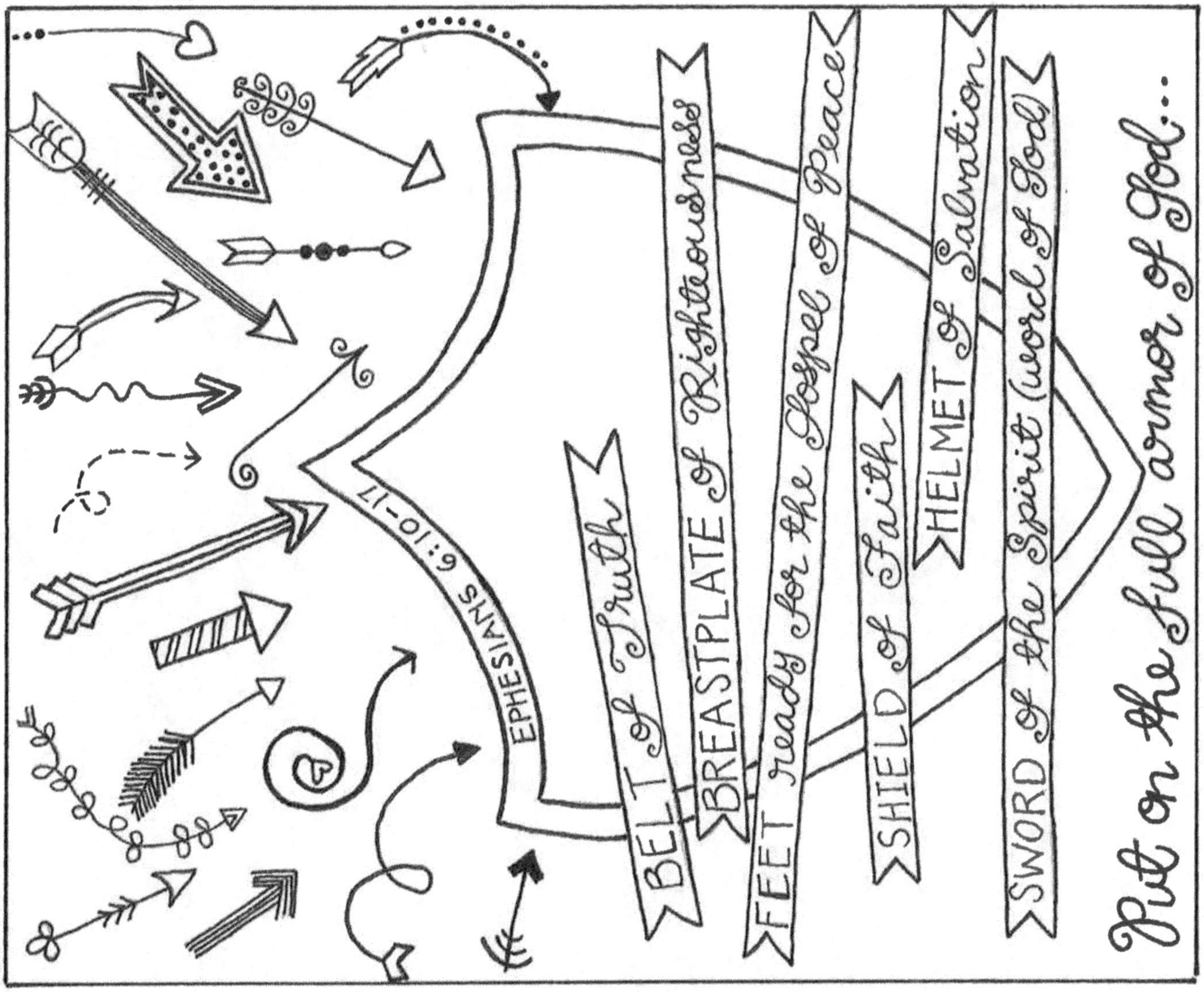

EPHESIANS 6:10-17

BELT of Truth

BREASTPLATE of Righteousness

FEET ready for the Gospel of Peace

SHIELD of Faith

HELMET of Salvation

SWORD of the Spirit (word of God)

Put on the full armor of God...

Who Are You?

by Lauren Reeves

Who are you? If I asked you this question, how would you reply? You might say, "I'm a banker." But that's not who you are. That's what you do for a living. So, WHO are you? You might say, "I'm a wife and a mother." And that's a piece of who you are right now, based on your reality of having a living husband and child. So, WHO are you: no matter what, all the time, in whatever role you're playing in life?

If you don't want to crumble when life shatters around you, you need to know who you are despite circumstances that can change and despite your ability to perform, which can also change.

My whole life I've identified with performance rather than who I really was deep down. I remember identifying as a "straight A student." If I couldn't live up to that identity one semester, my world fell apart. In my struggle to figure out who I was <u>again</u>, I threw myself into being a track star. I became an obsessed runner. I changed my diet in order to have more energy for races and completely cut out anything carbonated, since carbonation makes you short of breath. I ran to the point of stress-fractures in my feet, and when I rested from running, I read running magazines. Every time I won a race, I glided on an identity high. Plus, everyone loves a winner, right? But when I lost, I felt terrible about myself. I rode this rollercoaster until I graduated from high school and my days of being a track star ended.

In my struggle to figure out who I was <u>again</u>, I bought things and made things, led worship and counseled at camp, played guitar and wrote songs, and became friends with all sorts of different people to try to figure out what, or who, I wanted to be next. My soul was saved, but my heart was anxious and lost because I wasn't sure who I was, and honestly, I had never consulted God about this particular matter.

I graduated from college and started to work. I was good at my job, and I threw myself into it wholeheartedly. It was the perfect performance-based solution for my wandering identity. It was my career now, and I determined that my whole life was going to be devoted to it. I began climbing the proverbial ladder, yet my heart became more and more restless.

After years of working, I met a wonderful man and we got married. Soon after, he sensed my restless heart and suggested I quit my job and explore writing for the Lord. After I said yes and officially became unemployed, I realized there was a big problem. After I quit my job, it occurred to me that I didn't know the first thing about writing and my identity was lost again, leading me back down into that dark pit of self doubt.

I'm sad to say that it took years for God to convince me that my job wasn't who I was, and that He created me to be something more than a job. He created me to be more than a writer, even. He created me to be His. He created me to be valued and loved - an adopted daughter of the King with an inheritance that can never spoil or fade. He taught me that my identity shouldn't be in ANYTHING that can change. He is the only constant. He's the "Father of the heavenly lights, who does not change like shifting shadows" (James 1:17). He's "not a human being, that he should change His mind" (Numbers 23:19). He's "the same yesterday and today and forever" (Hebrews 13:8). And since He never changes, what He says about me can never change, spoil, or fade.

His Word tells you how you can know for certain you are His, and if you know for certain you are His, this is your identity: You are valuable and loved and nothing can separate you from His love (Jeremiah 31:3; Romans 8:35). You are established, anointed, and sealed by God - FOREVER His (2 Corinthians 1:21-22). You're His child (John 1:12). You are His friend (John 15:15). You are chosen by Christ to bear fruit (John 15:16). And these are just the fringes of your unshakeable identity! He declares you to be so much more than what I've listed here. For every shakable circumstance, He's given you an unshakable aspect of your identity. Know His Word. Who you are is all over those pages!

In Ephesians 6:12 Paul talks about our primary struggle in this life: "For our struggle is not against flesh and blood, but against the rulers, against the authorities, against the powers of this dark world and against the spiritual forces of evil in the heavenly realms." In other words, the Enemy is going to be after you every day of every week of every year of your life. He's going to try to lead you astray by making you believe you aren't who God says you are, and are not purposed for what He says you are. He tried it with Jesus, so we can expect he will do the same to us.

In Matthew 3, Jesus is baptized and when John raises Him out of the water, the Holy Spirit descends upon Him in the form of a dove. God then declares Jesus' identity for all to hear. "And a voice from heaven said, 'This is my Son, whom I love; with Him I am well pleased'" (Matthew 3:17). Immediately after this declaration, Jesus is led into the desert to be tempted by the devil for forty days. Guess what the Enemy uses to tempt Him? His identity! The first two times he tempts Jesus, he begins with, "If you are the Son of God…" The enemy tries to make us question our identity by insinuating that it HAS to be proven by our performance, or God's performance, or it can't be true. Let's read and see how the enemy works:

> The tempter came to Him and said, "*If You are the Son of God*, tell these stones to become bread."
> Jesus answered, "It is written: 'Man shall not live on bread alone, but on every word that comes from the mouth of God.'
> Then the devil took Him to the holy city and had Him stand on the highest point of the temple. "*If You are the Son of God*," he said, "throw Yourself down. For it is written:
>
> > 'He will command His angels concerning You, and they will lift You up in their hands, so that You will not strike Your foot against

a stone.'"

Jesus answered him, "It is also written: 'Do not put the Lord your God to the test.'" (Matthew 4:3-7, italics mine)

At Jesus' very recent baptism, Satan had heard the audible voice of God from heaven declaring that Jesus was the Son of God. Satan knew. He was trying to make <u>Jesus</u> question it. In my own life, the enemy does this same thing by saying, "Lauren, if you are child of God, then why can't you finish your book?" And, "Lauren, if you are loved by God, then why are you experiencing heartache again?" I fell into Satan's temptations many times before getting it right. But now that I recognize his mode of operation, my answers go more like this:

I AM a child of God and it is ok that I haven't finished my book because Philippians 2:13 says that it is God who works in me to will and to act in order to fulfill His good purpose. I've been praying and studying but keep getting stuck, so I'm resting in His leading. And Acts 17:26 says God marks out appointed times for everyone and everything, so I'm actively waiting upon Him but ultimately trusting His timing.

And, Satan, I AM loved by God. I'm experiencing heartache again because I live in a fallen world caused by YOU and YOUR lies (Genesis 3:4). But I also know that if my heartache is discipline, then my God disciplines those He loves (Hebrews 12:6), and if my heartache is suffering, I count it joy when I face trials because it produces perseverance in me (James 1:2-3).

If our identities are firmly rooted in the unshakable Word of God, then they cannot be shaken. And Jesus knew the Enemy would try to confuse what we know to be true about ourselves. Look what Jesus prayed for us right before He went to the cross: "My prayer is not that you take them out of the world but that you protect them from the evil one. They are not of this world, even as I am not of it. Sanctify them by the truth; your word is truth" (John 17:15-17). Even in His prayer for us, He recognizes our power against the evil one is truth, unshakable truth from the Word of God!

Learn to identify with who you really are. Your performances will fall short, He won't always prove Himself to you (Isn't that why it's called faith?), and your circumstances will prove to be ever changing. Rest your identity in the place it was always meant to be – in who God says you are.

1. Before reading this, how would you have answered, "Who are you?"

2. Have you ever identified yourself with your performance? If so, how?

3. What is God's character according to James 1:17, Numbers 23:19, and Hebrews 13:8? Therefore, what is your unshakeable identity according to Romans 8:35, Jeremiah 31:3, 2 Corinthians 1:21-22, John 1:12, John 15:15, and John 15:16?

4. Are there any other verses, hymns, or songs that help remind you about who you are in Christ?

5. The Enemy can feed us negative lies concerning who we are, which breeds insecurity and, therefore, keeps us from attempting what God has asked of us. On the flip side, the Enemy can stroke our ego and abilities, which births pride in us and, therefore, tempts us to serve God in our own flesh and confidence in ourselves rather than in Him. Can you identify specific ways the Enemy might be doing this right now in your life?

6. In the last part of the devotional, I wrote out an example of how I address the Enemy when he's trying to discourage me or tempt me to believe something false. Based on your answer to #5 and what you know to be true about you from God's Word, how can you respond to the Enemy? Write your answer below.
   I've provided a list of scripture references on the next two pages that describe your identity in Christ. Feel free to use those to help you construct your answer.

Who Am I?
Scripture References About My Identity in Christ

ACCEPTANCE

Jeremiah 31:3 – I am loved by God with an everlasting and faithful love.

John 1:12 – I am a child of God.

John 15:15 – I am a friend of Christ.

Romans 5:1 – I have been declared righteous by faith and, therefore, have peace with God through Jesus.

1 Corinthians 3:16 – I am God's temple and His Spirit lives in me.

1 Corinthians 6:17 – I am joined to the Lord.

1 Corinthians 6:19-20 – I am a temple for the Holy Spirit. I am not my own. I am God's.

1 Corinthians 12:27 – I am a member of the body of Christ.

2 Corinthians 2:15 – I am the fragrance of Christ to people.

Ephesians 1:1 – I am a saint because of Christ Jesus.

Ephesians 1:5 – I am adopted as God's child.

Ephesians 2:18 – I have direct access to God through the Holy Spirit.

Colossians 1:13 – I am a citizen in the kingdom of the Son.

Colossians 1:14 – I am redeemed and forgiven.

Colossians 1:22 – I have been reconciled through Christ's death and am holy, faultless, and blameless before Him.

Colossians 2:7 – I am rooted and built up in Christ.

Colossians 2:10 – I am filled by Christ.

Hebrews 2:11 – I am being sanctified.

SECURITY

Romans 8:1-2 – I am not condemned. I am free from the law of sin and death.

Romans 8:17 – I am an heir of God and co-heir with Christ.

Romans 8:28 – I am called to His purpose, so He works all things together for my good.

Romans 8:31-34 – I am God's elect. He is for me, not against me, and Jesus intercedes for me.

Romans 8:35-39 – I cannot be separated from the love of Christ.

2 Corinthians 1:21-22 – I am strengthened, anointed, and sealed by God.

Philippians 1:6 – I am worth enough to Him that He promises not to give up on me.

Philippians 3:20 – I am a citizen of heaven.

Philippians 4:19 – I am taken care of by God.

Colossians 3:3 – I am hidden with Christ in God.

2 Timothy 1:7 – I don't have to be insecure. I am given power, love, and self discipline by the Spirit.

Hebrews 4:16 – I can be confident, because of Jesus, that I can approach God and will receive mercy and grace to help me in my time of need.

1 John 5:18 – I am safe because of Jesus, and the evil one cannot harm me.

SIGNIFICANCE

Matthew 5:13-14 – I am the salt of the earth and the light of the world.

John 15:1, 5 – I will bear much fruit as long as I abide in Christ.

John 15:16 – I was chosen and appointed that I might bear fruit that will last. So I will be given whatever I ask the Father for in Jesus' name.

Acts 1:8 – I am given power to be His witness because of the Holy Spirit.

Romans 5:19 – I am made righteous because of the obedience of Jesus.

1 Corinthians 3:9 – I am a co-worker in God's service. I am part of the field He is growing fruit in. I am part of His building He is constructing on the foundation of Jesus.

1 Corinthians 3:16 – I am God's temple where His Spirit dwells.

2 Corinthians 5:17-21 – I am part of the new creation and have been given the ministry or reconciliation. I am therefore Christ's ambassador.

2 Corinthians 6:1 – I am God's co-worker.

Ephesians 2:6 – I am seated with Christ in the heavenly realms.

Ephesians 2:10 – I am God's masterpiece, created in Christ Jesus to do good works, which were prepared in advance for me to do.

Ephesians 3:12 – With faith in Jesus, I can approach God with freedom and confidence.

Philippians 4:13 – I can do all things through Him who gives me strength.

Colossians 3:12 – I am chosen, holy, and dearly loved by God, so I will clothe myself with compassion, kindness, humility, gentleness, and patience.

Hebrews 3:1 – I share in the heavenly calling, so I will fix my thoughts on Jesus.

James 1:5 – I can ask God for wisdom and He will generously give it to me.

1 Peter 2:5 – I am like a living stone being built together with other living stones into a spiritual house to be a holy priesthood, offering spiritual sacrifices acceptable to God through Christ Jesus.

1 Peter 2:9-10 – Other true believers and I are His chosen people, a royal priesthood, a holy nation, and God's special possession. So I will declare the praises of Him who called me out of darkness into His wonderful light!

lettering #3

A B C D E
F G H i J K
L M N O P
Q R S T U
V W X Y Z

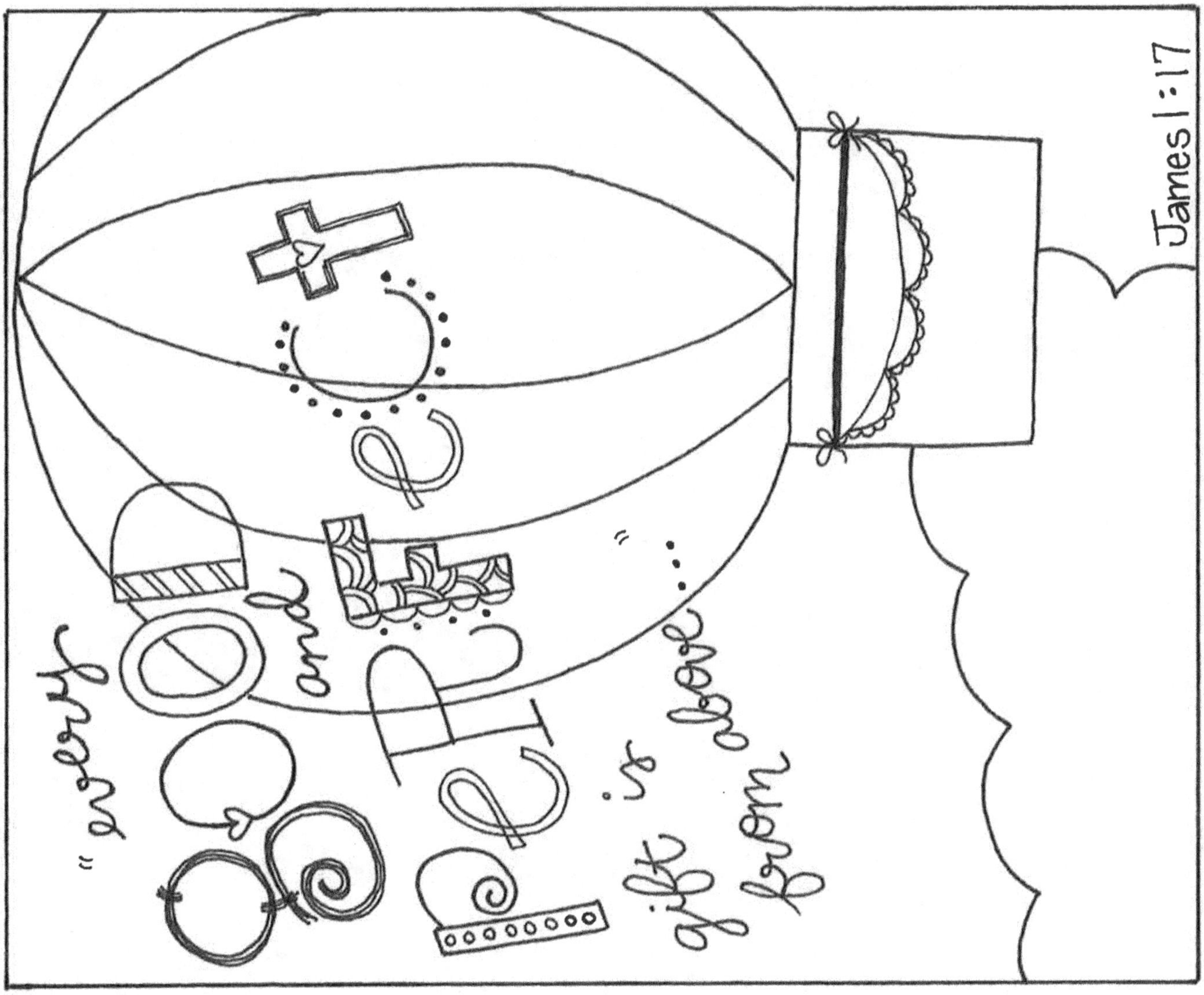

"Every good and perfect gift is from above"
James 1:17

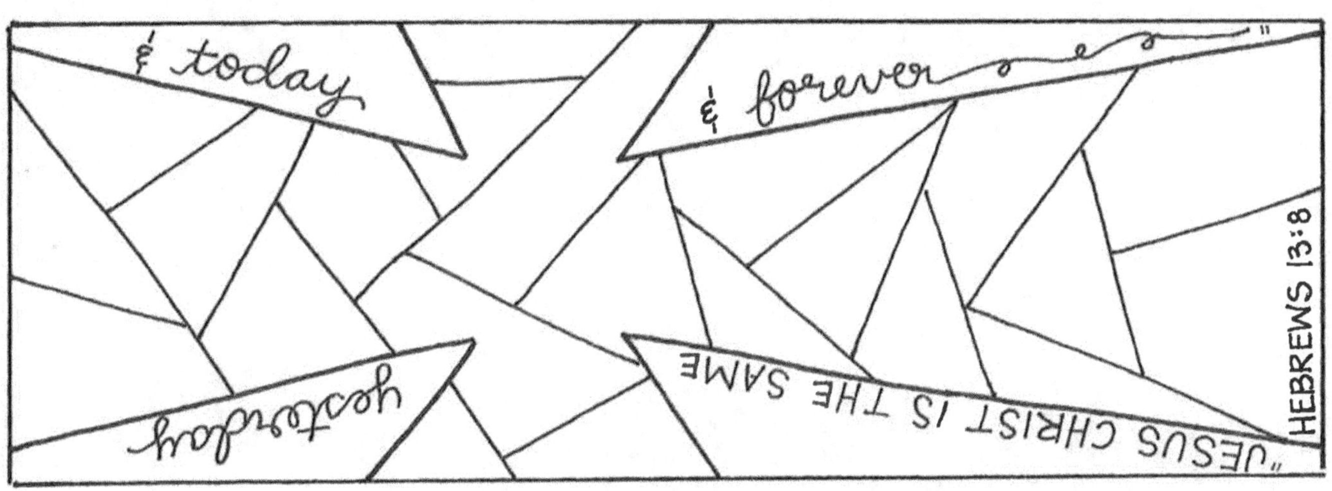
& today
yesterday
& forever
"JESUS CHRIST IS THE SAME
HEBREWS 13:8

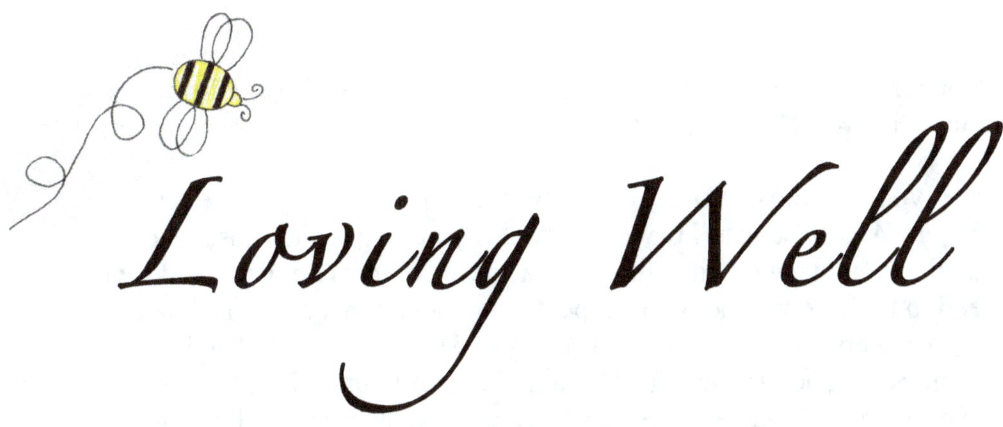

Loving Well

by Lauren Reeves

When I think about my journey of relationships, I realize that misunderstandings and miscommunications happen so easily. And, as a Christian, have you noticed that wounds from other believers seem to pierce deeper and are even more confusing than if they were from unbelievers? When it's God's people who have hurt you, the betrayal seems deeper; the hurt seems more hurtful; and the rejection feels more personal. It doesn't line up with our expectations. But it happens. No matter how careful you are, it seems to happen to one degree or another eventually. The questions of survival become: Who's the most resilient? Who's willing to persevere when a relationship gets tough? And who is willing to navigate the muddy waters of reconciliation?

The truth is, you can experience such pain and trauma in your life that you determine, whether consciously or subconsciously, to never allow yourself to be hurt again.   You stop loving. You stop letting yourself be known and loved. You build walls and your heart grows cold.

Jesus, speaking of the days I believe we are in right now, said, "Then many will take offense, betray one another and hate one another… Because lawlessness will multiply, the love of many will grow cold. But the one who endures to the end will be delivered" (Matthew 24:10,12, HCSB). He warns us that our hearts will take quite a beating and yet the two greatest commandments remain the same: "'Love the Lord Your God with all your heart and with all your soul and with all your mind.' This is the first and greatest commandment. And the second is like it: 'Love your neighbor as yourself.' All the Law and the Prophets hang on these two commandments" (Matthew 22:37-40).

A lot of us say, "Well I love God. I just can't trust people enough to love them." When we get to that point (and I have been there), we are deceiving ourselves, because 1 John 4:20 says, "Whoever claims to love God yet hates a brother or sister is a liar. For whoever does not love their brother and sister whom they have seen, cannot love God, whom they have not seen."

Christianity is set apart as the only religion with a foundation of love. Other religions are founded upon being a good person or on disciplining yourself to be this way or that way. Love is the essence of Christianity and yet many of us have become "love-shy." We are fearful to receive love, and even when love is genuine, we are distrustful. And we are fearful to give committed, no-matter-what kind of love. The temptation is to only love with the kind of love that says, "I'll love you if you love me and don't hurt me. But if you hurt me, I'm out!"

The problem is, that is how the world loves. This kind of shallow love makes us no different than the world. Jesus says:

> If you love those who love you, what credit is that to you? Even sinners love those who love them. And if you do good to those who are good to you, what credit is that to you? Even sinners do that. And if you lend to those from whom you expect repayment, what credit is that to you? Even sinners lend to sinners, expecting to be repaid in full. But love your enemies, do good to them, and lend to them without expecting to get anything back. Then your reward will be great, and you will be children of the Most High, because he is kind to the ungrateful and wicked. Be merciful, just as your Father is merciful. (Luke 6:32-36)

Because the basis of God's Will for our lives is love, it's important that we learn to live in love and persevere in love as well. But we CAN'T do this consistently on our own. We have to be changed from the inside out…. constantly… by our Maker.

The prophet Ezekiel spoke of the new covenant we have in Christ when he spoke for God saying, "I will give you a new heart and put a new spirit in you; I will remove from you your heart of stone and give you a heart of flesh. And I will put my Spirit in you and move you to follow my decrees and be careful to keep my laws" (Ezekiel 36:26-27). He removes our hearts of stone and gives us hearts that are soft toward Him and His ways. And I love that it says the Holy Spirit MOVES you to follow His decrees. God softens your heart and the Spirit inside you MOVES your heart to love the way only He can!

So, obviously, we NEED to continually come before God, allowing Him to keep our hearts soft, and we NEED the Holy Spirit to have the freedom in our lives to MOVE us to love well. First Thessalonians 5:19 says, "Do not quench the Spirit," but instead, as Ephesians 5:18 says, "be filled with the Spirit." A more literal translation of the original language in Ephesians 5:18 would be "be filled with the Spirit over and over and over again." The command to be filled with the Spirit doesn't imply that we can lose the Spirit, but we can certainly quench Him and have varying degrees of evidence of Him in our lives.

I've heard it explained like this: Imagine a series of pipe works running through your soul. The main pipe begins at your heart and then branches off to every other area of your life. The Holy Spirit is always in the main pipe of your heart after salvation, but He has to be invited and allowed to fill the branches everyday. We can actually block Him from filling areas of our soul. The Spirit can be quenched by our pride, unconfessed sin, arrogance, independence, etc. On the other hand, we can allow Him to fill every area as we surrender all aspects of our lives to His control, hide His Word in our hearts, and go to Him consistently in prayer. Being filled with the Spirit is a daily choice. We can choose to do things our own way and make our own plans, and the Spirit is quenched. Or, we can totally surrender, put our eyes on Him, and be filled with the Spirit to a greater degree.

David, the man after God's own heart, involved God in every area of his life. He penned the words we've heard so often: "Cast your cares on the Lord and He will sustain you; He will never let the righteous be shaken" (Psalm 55:22). But do you know in what context these words were written? They were written in the midst of hurt and betrayal by a close friend – one who had walked with him at the house of God.

David RAN to God when his heart was hurting. He RAN to God to tell Him all his troubles. He was open and honest and knew that God was the ONLY one that could bind up his broken heart. Let's read a little about his pain in Psalm 55:

> If an enemy were insulting me,
>   I could endure it;
> If a foe were rising against me,
>   I could hide.
> But it is you, a man like myself,
>   my companion, my close friend,
> with whom I once enjoyed sweet fellowship
>   at the house of God,
> as we walked about
>   among the worshipers…
>
> As for me, I call to God,
>   and the Lord saves me.
> Evening, morning and noon
>   I cry out in distress,
>   and He hears my voice. (Psalm 55:12-14, 16-17)

Evening, morning and noon he cried out in distress to his God who heard his voice. Don't you love that? It shows how intimately involved God was allowed to be in his life.

God has been teaching me that I would never have known Him as I do if I hadn't suffered, and then struggled with Him in prayer about my suffering. God didn't exempt His own Son from suffering. Jesus was without sin, yet He "learned obedience from what he suffered" (Hebrews 5:8). He was made perfect "through what He suffered" (Hebrews 2:10). Why shouldn't we expect the same?

He uses suffering to refine us and make us more equipped to bring Him glory with our lives. And that's the heart cry of everyone I know who truly loves Jesus. So wouldn't it make sense that He could use our hurt to produce that in us?

You WILL get hurt if you choose to love people and let them into your life. David got hurt. Paul and Barnabas hurt each other (Acts 15:39). I have been, and you will be. We can't take the good and not the bad. The bad is what sharpens us and makes us beautiful if we take it to the Master Refiner. So love well without fear of suffering. He can make the darkest nights into the most glorious mornings.

"As iron sharpens iron, so one person sharpens another" (Proverbs 27:17).

Discussion Questions

1. If you've ever been hurt in a relationship, how did it affect you going forward?

2. When you hurt, who do you run to first? Does this need to change?

3. Has God ever used pain as an opportunity to draw you closer to Him? How can
    this turn our feelings from hurt to love?

4. Write out Matthew 22:37-40. Emphasize the important words in these verses.

5. How can we pray for you to "love well" if you've been hurt recently?

Lettering #4

A B C D E F G H I J K L M
N O P Q R S J U V W X Y Z
0 1 2 3 4 5 6 7 8 9

a b c d e f g h i j k l m n o p q r
s t u v w x y z
! ? $ % # @

be kind · HONOR · Joy
grow

direction

abcdefghijkLmnop
qrstuvwxyz

happy hope hello heart

mercies go bright

Smile

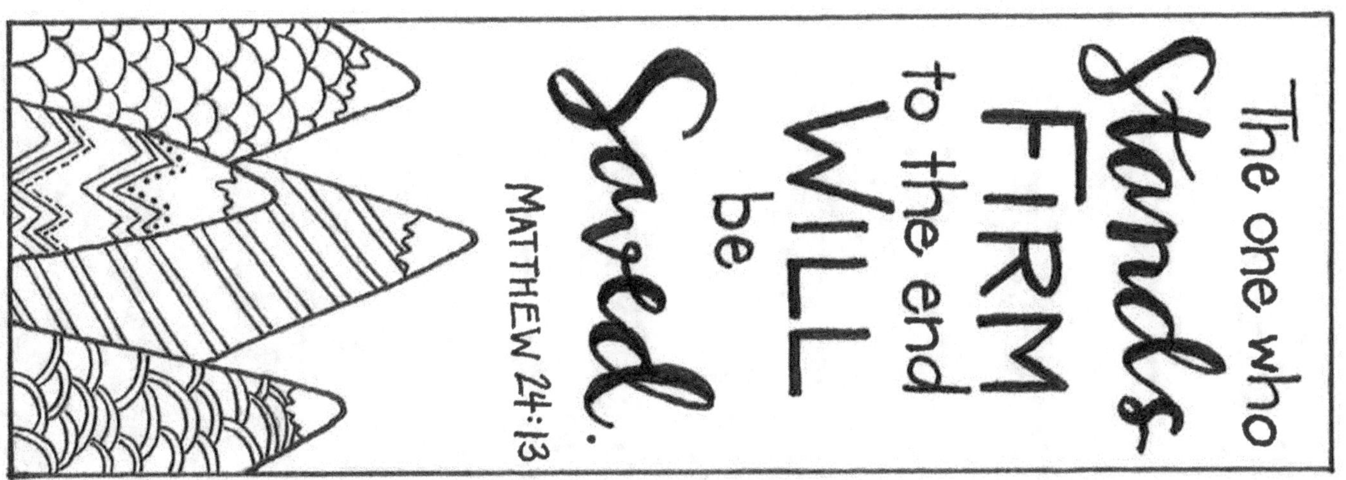

The one who
Stands FIRM
to the end
WILL
be
Saved.
MATTHEW 24:13

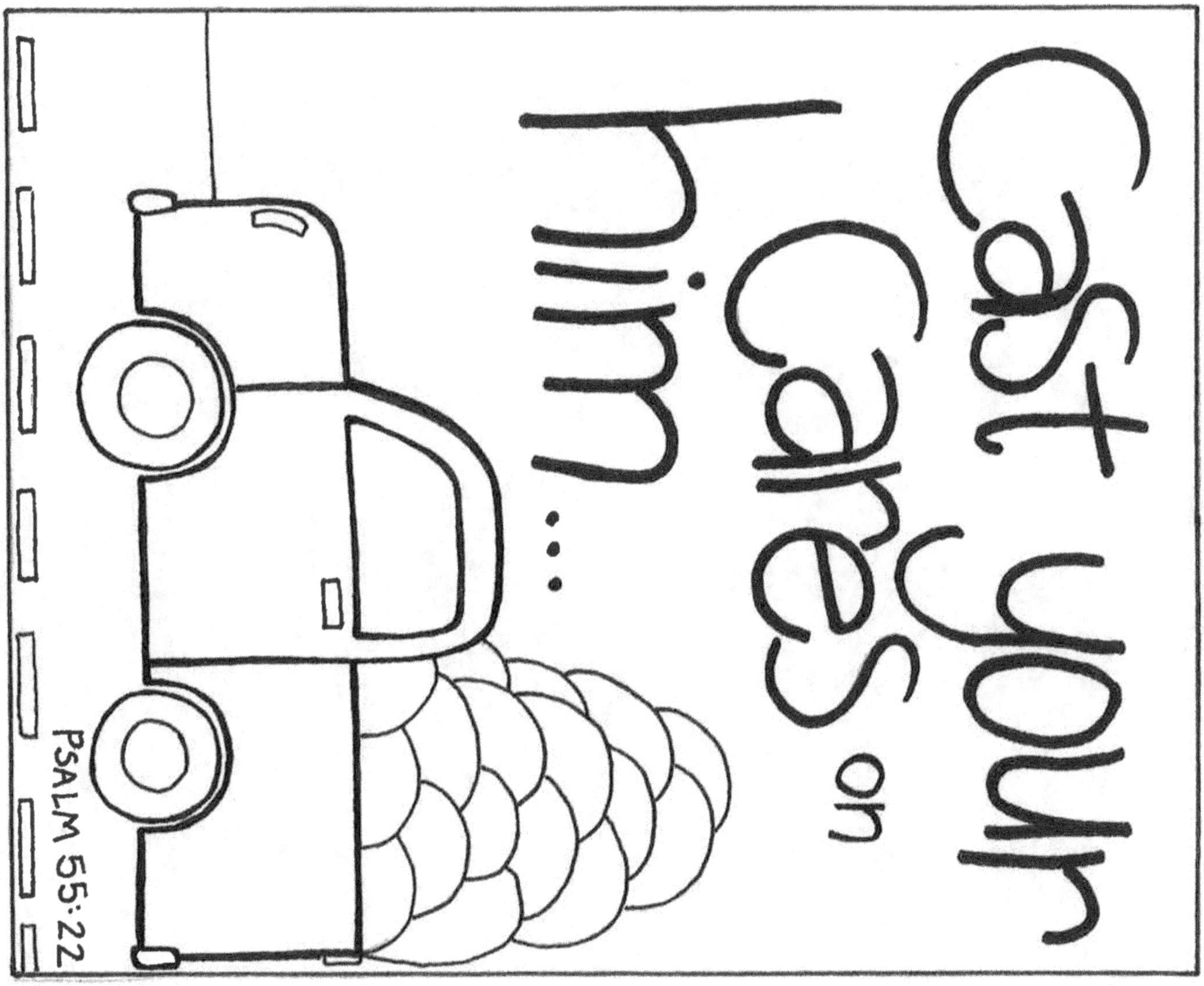

Cast your
Cares on
him ...
PSALM 55:22

Abide in Me

by Lauren Reeves

How we think God views us can determine how close we allow ourselves to be to Him. I'm convinced of this. We are wired for these two things to correlate. For example, if you really like someone and discover they like you as well, you naturally like them even more and draw a little closer to them. On the flip side, what happens when you like someone but you think they dislike you? It's hard to believe there's a chance that relationship will work out, isn't it? People don't continue to pursue or cultivate relationships like that for long. In the same way, how we think God views us can determine how much we are willing to draw near to Him.

If you made a list with words or phrases that describe how you think God views you, would it include mostly negative or positive thoughts? There have been times in my Christian walk when I believed I had failed God, or that He was disappointed in me, or that He was mad at me because I hadn't done enough for Him. Those thoughts made me want to hide from Him, and any time spent seeking Him through Bible study and prayer slipped away from me. But I can tell you from experience, you CAN overcome the insecurity you may feel in approaching God, even if it's a subconscious insecurity you've never identified but has ruled your spiritual life.

Here's the truth: Because of the finished work of Jesus, in whatever season you may find yourself, Hebrews 4:16 says we can "approach the throne of grace with confidence, so that we may receive mercy and find grace to help us in our time of need." Stand against the condemnation you feel because of how you may think God views you. That's the enemy at work in your mind, trying to keep you away from the truth that you're hidden in Christ and, therefore, forgiven! He's crazy about you and wants to partner with you!

In fact, He wants us to want to be with Him all the time! For all of you "quality time" people out there, this should speak to His love for you! John 15:4 says, "Abide in Me" (ESV). A few verses later, He says it slightly differently, "Abide in My love" (John 15:9, ESV). I like that. The truth is, if you get this one right, He will work everything else out in you, including His Will for your life. In this section of scripture, Jesus is described as the Vine and we are described as branches. We are branches who cannot bear fruit or live apart from the Vine. However, when we are connected to the Vine, the Living Water of life is allowed to flow through our veins, enabling us to grow and bear fruit for the Kingdom.

So, how do we abide? We have to come to view our nearness to Him as our source of life. Seeking to understand His Word and praying are two ways that help us draw near. When you were "born again," you were given a new sense of God's presence and love, and the Spirit to guide and strengthen you. But just like a baby, this sense needs nurturing and developing. You have to learn to hear the Spirit and you have to grow in your knowledge of His presence and love. If you don't nurture this sense, your flesh will eventually take over again, quenching the Spirit, and luring you to live no differently than before. That's powerless living for the Kingdom. It's a war to overcome your flesh. Your flesh had years of training before you came to salvation. For most of us, the crucial childhood developmental years were lived learning desires and ways of the flesh ("give me," "I want," "it's not fair"). We have to nurture our new self in Christ to allow it to grow stronger than our flesh. But don't get me wrong. Prayer and Bible study should not be a legalistic, beat-yourself-up-if-you-miss-a-day kind of thing. Remember, we are also given freedom and unearned favor because of Christ! But, overall consistency of both in your life will quicken your ears to hear His voice leading, loving, and guiding you.

The more you taste Him, the more you will grow to hunger and thirst for Him. That's how we begin to remain in the Vine. Confess anything that might be hindering you from coming to Him and then continually taste Him through Bible study and prayer. You'll wake up one day and realize you crave Him and can't live without Him.

Paul talks of the need for self-discipline in the faith in 1 Corinthians 9:24-27. And it's true. There is a need for that in our faith, but people prefer to not talk about it. Our relationship with God, like any close relationship, takes time and consistency in order to keep it alive and vibrant. I have yet to find a strong Christian who doesn't consistently read his or her Bible. Do you know why? Because once we are saved, we are as close to God as we choose to be. Once we are saved, He calls us deeper than just a salvation experience. But, do we respond? Christians who are strong in their faith have chosen to respond and draw near to God consistently through prayer, worship, and Bible study, abiding in Him as their source of spiritual life.

James 4:8 says, "Draw near to God, and He will draw near to you" (ESV). That's a promise. But let me be clear. God's nearness does not always or even often mean that we will feel Him. We live in a culture that is all about the next thrilling experience. Sadly, even many in our churches have inadvertently led believers to think we will feel Him if He's close. If we don't feel Him, something must be wrong. But, the truth is, God often calls us to walk by faith. In fact, Hebrews 11:9 says, "Without faith, it is impossible to please God."

In his book, *Real Church*, Larry Crabb tells the following story about his father's faith:

> After he had open-heart surgery that led to two long weeks of life-threatening complications and kept him in the hospital, I was driving him home to recuperate. From the backseat, my seventy-nine-year-old father, lying down as best he could, broke a sober silence by quietly saying, "You know, I had many visitors during my difficult hospital stay, and I appreciated every one. But the one visitor I most wanted to come never showed up."
>
> "Who?" I asked with real curiosity.
>
> "God," he answered. "I prayed every day that I would feel His presence. I never did. And I'm so grateful."
>
> "Why?" I blurted out, this time with wild curiosity.

"God counted me worthy to trust what He said in His Word in the absence of His felt presence in my experience. And His Spirit empowered me to do just that, not without struggle of course. But I never turned away from Him. I think that made Him really happy."[1]

To trust in God's Word over what I see or feel is hard. I'm a very sensitive and emotional person deep down. I love that I feel deeply when it's good, but I hate that I feel deeply when it's bad. I have felt the Lord's presence and been overwhelmed with the ways He makes me feel loved. I've been inspired by the mysteries He sometimes reveals to me in His Word and can ride that rush for days! Feeling God is like my drug. I crave it. And when I don't feel Him, I'm like doubting Thomas. I want God to constantly demonstrate His presence rather than trusting His presence is there regardless.

The story of doubting Thomas in John 20:24-31 is my favorite and yet it's one I struggle with constantly. Jesus had died, been buried in the tomb, and was now resurrected in His new body, walking around appearing to the people. The disciples ran to Thomas to tell him, "We have seen the Lord!" But Thomas couldn't believe it, even though Jesus had told him before He died that He would be raised to life. Thomas said to them, "Unless I see the nail marks in his hands and put my finger where the nails were, and put my hand into his side, I will not believe it." A week later Jesus showed Himself to Thomas and let him put his finger in His side and see His nail scarred hands. It was THEN that Thomas truly believed. What Jesus said next is the part that gets me. Jesus told him, "Because you have seen me, you have believed; blessed are those who have not seen and yet have believed."

God has used this in my life to say, "Lauren, do you need Me to prove Myself to you AGAIN? Or do you want to be considered blessed for believing even though you don't see or feel me at times?" So I choose to read even when I don't feel Him in it. I choose to pray even when I don't feel Him…or at least try. And y'all, just the act of STARTING to pray is hard! Our thoughts can so easily be led astray from prayer and onto everything else we have going on.

Here's a technique that helps me focus in times of prayer: Pick a place where you can get alone. Open your Bible and start reading. Keep a notepad close by to jot down anything the passage may be telling you about the character of God, or what He can do or promises to do. You can also search the qualities of God, Jesus, or the Holy Spirit in your concordance. Then begin your prayers by praying those things. For example, if my passage for the day included the verses about the fruit of the Spirit (Galatians 5:22-23), I could choose one and make that the theme of my opening prayer. It might start something like this:

God, one of the fruits of your Spirit is gentleness. I know in order to bear the fruit of gentleness in our lives, You Yourself have to first be gentle since You are the source of that - and You ARE gentle. I've seen how you're gentle with me when my feelings are hurt and how you comfort me with the comfort of your presence when I run to You in those times of pain. Your Word even says you put

---

[1] Taken from *Real Church: Does It Exist? Can I Find It?* by Larry Crabb Copyright © 2009 by Larry Crabb. Used by permission of Thomas Nelson. www.thomasnelson.com

*all my tears in a jar and not one of them is forgotten. Thank You for being so kind
and gentle and loving to me.*

By this time in the prayer, you have overcome the hardest part, which is starting. This
technique takes away the hurdle of trying to figure out how to start praying. Then just let
your prayer flow from there. You can ask Him to show you His heart in situations in
your life; you can listen; you can beg; you can confess; you can turn on music and
worship. He loves your creativity, so just take it from there and let it go wherever He
leads. The important thing is making sure we allow our mind and heart to connect to the
Vine consistently.

Bible study = growth; prayer = power. You wouldn't want to grow in knowledge but
have no power from the Spirit. That could be like "having a form of godliness but
denying its power" (2 Timothy 3:5). But at the same time, you wouldn't want to just
pray without reading His Word or your passion might outrun your wisdom and
understanding. We need both to be healthy and well-rounded spiritually.

The more we understand His Word and experience the power He brings to our lives
through prayer, the more confident we become in Christ's love and support and the more
we trust what His Word says over what we see or feel. That's abiding in Him.

Discussion Questions

1. Before reading this devotional, how did you believe God viewed you? Be honest.

2. Read these verses and write beside each one how God truly sees us:

John 1:12

Hebrews 8:12

2 Corinthians 5:17

Ephesians 4:24

Matthew 5:14

Ephesians 2:10

3. Look up the definition of "abide" and write it here.

4. Have you ever falsely understood that the presence of God will always be associated with a feeling or experience? Although, His presence can be a wonderful feeling and experience at times, what parts of our secular or church culture made you feel it should <u>always</u> be that way if you were "doing it right?"

5. Read Matthew 18:20. What does Jesus' assurance in this verse tell us? Will His presence always be obvious (i.e. a feeling or experience)?

We would love to see your Sketching Scripture art each week. If you post your completed Bible journaling art on social media, use our hashtag so we can find you!
#sketchingscripture

Lettering #5

add interest
to the letters
(bottom left)

A B C D E F G H I J K
L M N O P Q R S T U
V W X Y Z

DRAW NEAR
FAITH . HOPE . LOVE .

LIGHT   STARS

RESCUED

REJOICE always

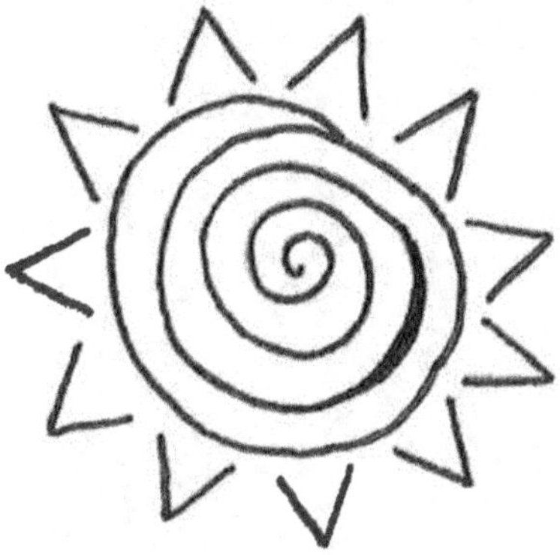

HI

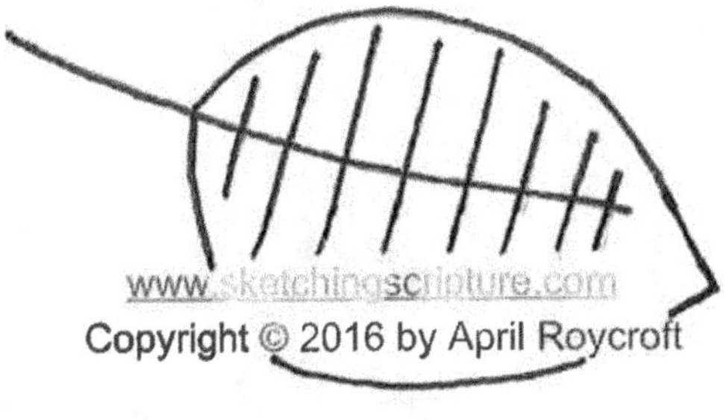

www.sketchingscripture.com

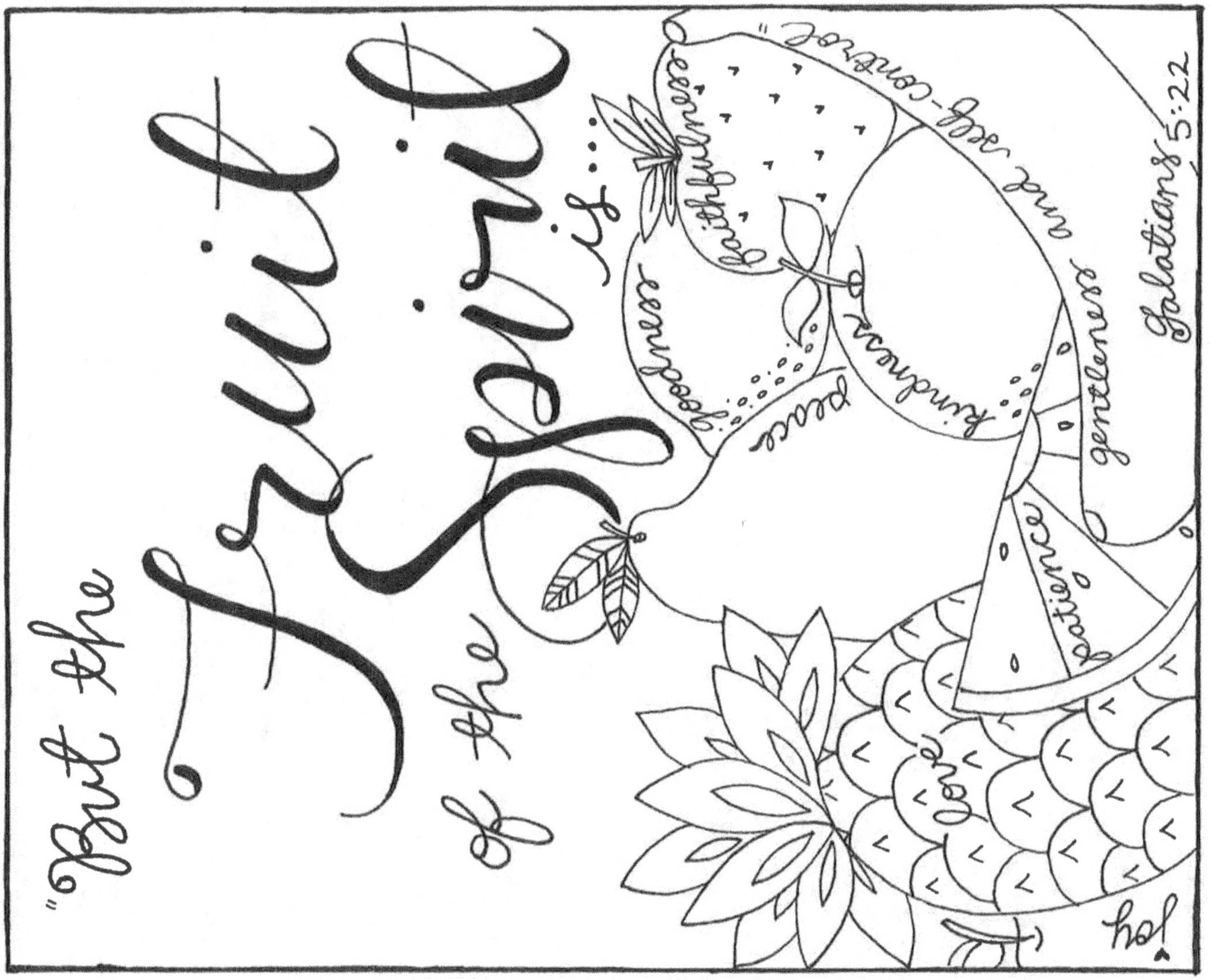

"But the fruit of the Spirit is... of the

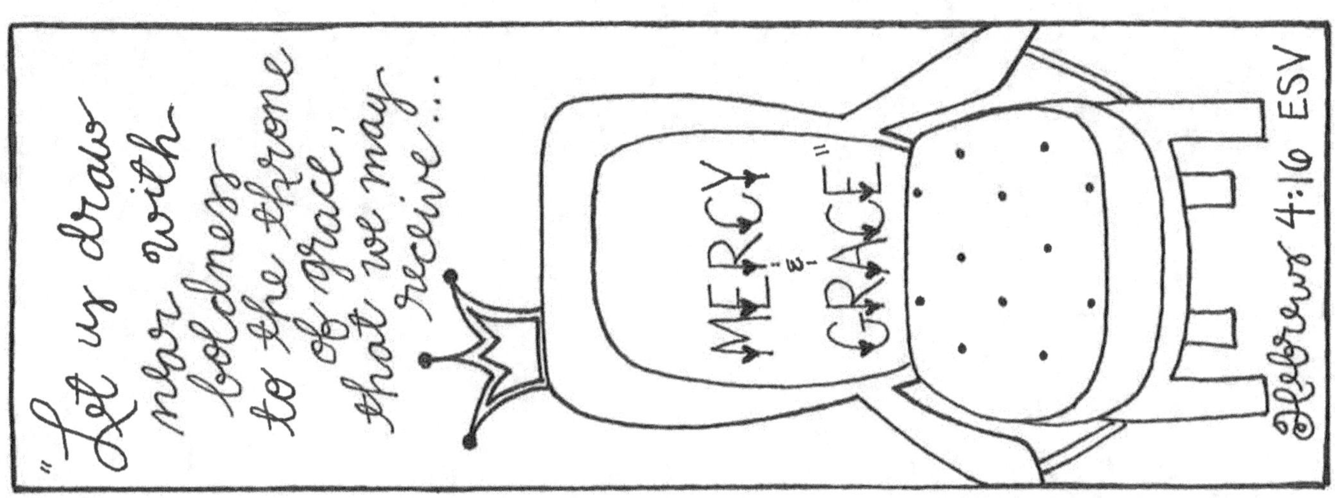

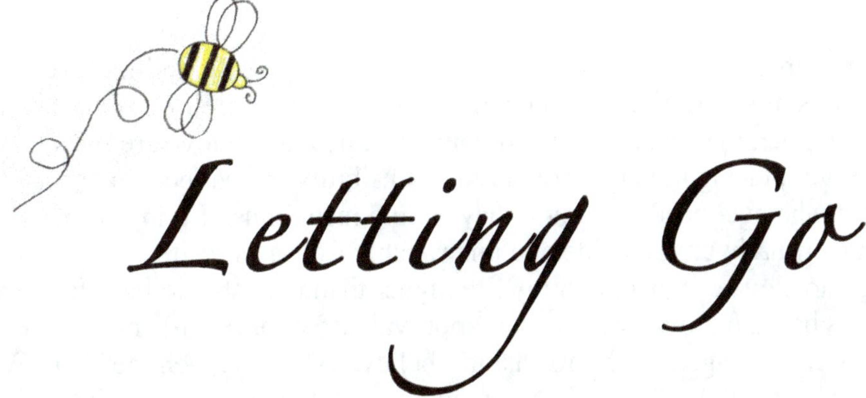

Letting Go

by Lauren Reeves

I saw a post on Instagram the other day. I've actually seen it posted a lot with no credit given to whoever was the original author. It's as if it's a second-nature catch phrase. The post said, "Some people come into your life just to teach you how to let go." Do you ever look back and feel that way about some of your past relationships, especially if you held onto them too desperately or allowed them to occupy the highest place in your life? No one can stand on that pedestal for long without falling. I've seen it played out in my life several times. God can use the repetition of that scenario to discipline us (as a Good Father does) in order to teach us we were made to love Him far above anyone or anything else.

Loving God most is what is good for me, and that's the command I'm designed to thrive under. But I want something or someone I can see. I want an audible voice that can talk back to me and arms that can hug me. I think I long for those things first because that's how we will be with God one day. It's just that for now there's this chasm keeping us from seeing, touching, and audibly hearing Him. It's a faith journey for now. And maybe having faith in and love for One who's real but unseen authenticates our love in a greater, deeper way. All I know is the struggle is real to keep God first in my life! And I'm not the only one.

The Israelites struggled with it while Moses was up on Mount Sinai meeting with God. Apparently, Moses was taking too long and so they took it upon themselves to make a golden calf to worship (Exodus 32). They wanted something they could see and touch rather than faith in Someone they couldn't.

Solomon struggled with it when he sought out 700 wives and 300 concubines (1 Kings 11:3) in order to make himself happy rather than seeking God. Side note: To me, the craziest part about Solomon is the fact that he had 700 wives and 300 concubines, and yet God had given him the wisdom to actually write Song of Solomon in the Bible – a book which is about the beauty of the love of ONE man and ONE woman! Sadly, Solomon didn't choose to live most of his life within the wisdom God gave him. Isn't that often the case for us, too? God will go to great lengths to give us wisdom about a certain situation, yet we still choose to reject that wisdom.

It never fails. When I begin to love a friend or a dream or an achievement even close to the degree to which I love God, for one reason or another, that friend, dream, or achievement fails me or crumbles out of my life. The pain of this loss drives me deeper into His love and makes me realize, once again, God is the only one who is completely constant and the only one who has true, unfailing love. I should know this by now. In fact, did you know that every time the Bible mentions the phrase "unfailing love" or a love that never fails, it is referring to God's love, not man's? Therefore, if our hearts are first filled by God, then the achievements, dreams, and people we love are just a really fun bonus. We stop placing the high-pressure responsibility on that person or idea to fulfill us or meet whatever needs we think they should meet in us. Living within His way, we become virtually unshakeable and unswayable from His Will.

When I begin to elevate someone in my life higher than they should be, I find myself making decisions based on my need for their approval, affection, or affirmation. I have thoughts like, "Will they agree with this vision I believe God has given me?" or "What will [insert name here] think of me if I obey God but look like a fool doing it?" The people pleaser in me might think something like, "I can't tell [insert name here] what He's nudging me to tell her! What if she gets mad at me?!" Do you see how fragile my faith and obedience become when I position people higher than they should be in my life? My decision to obey God becomes harder because I'm viewing it through the lens of what I fear or assume that person thinks, which is most often simply a guess.

When Jesus was talking to a large crowd, He said to them, "If anyone comes to Me and does not hate father and mother, wife and children, brothers and sisters – yes, even their own life – such a person cannot be my disciple. And whoever does not carry their cross and follow Me cannot be my disciple" (Luke 14:25-27). We know that in this passage of scripture Jesus wasn't asking the people to be hateful to each other. He had told His disciples that to love God with all your heart, mind, soul, and strength and to love your neighbor as yourself were the two greatest commandments (Mark 12:30-31). He was demonstrating in his speech that your love for God should be so great that your love for the people closest to you and the love you have for your own life should look like hate in comparison. Y'all, that's hard. But the longer I live, the more this lesson is shaping me and actually making me feel more complete. It's strange. It's hard to understand, but I'm learning that it's best.

I think our view about the decision to follow Christ gets a little bit skewed living in America. We all want "to go to heaven when we die," so naturally, we want to identify with Christianity, but not many of us have actually counted the cost. Several times in scripture people tell Jesus they want to follow Him. Look through your Bible and try to find a time where Jesus' response was, "Oh, thank you! Now, I shall reward you with a happy, problem-free life, nice cars, successful careers, and kids that are good at sports!" No! He never says that! Not even anything close to that! Luke 9:57-62 says:

> As they were walking along the road, a man said to Him, "I will follow You wherever You go."
>
> Jesus replied, "Foxes have dens and birds have nests, but the Son of Man has no place to lay His head."
>
> He said to another man, "Follow Me."
>
> But he replied, "Lord, first let me go and bury my father."
>
> Jesus said to him, "Let the dead bury their own dead, but you go and proclaim the kingdom of God."
>
> Still another said, "I will follow You, Lord; but first let me go back and say goodbye to my family."

> Jesus replied, "No one who puts a hand to the plow and looks back is
> fit for service in the kingdom of God."

Ouch. That's serious. Where do we get off thinking Christianity is a casual faith we can just tack onto our week? It's actually a wholly committed love relationship that ends up transforming your entire life and purpose for living. And He very rarely ends up leading you the way YOU had planned (I'm sensing anxiety in all the Type-A personalities after that last sentence). I guess this is the point He was trying to make when He said, "Whoever wants to be My disciple must deny themselves and take up their cross and follow Me. For whoever wants to save their life will lose it, but whoever loses their life for me will find it" (Matthew 16:24-25). This is the kind of commitment that forfeits our own plans in honor of working toward His greater plan, reveres obedience to Him over what others may think or ask, and is even willing to lay down our physical life if necessary.

Jesus made this statement about our commitment to follow Him: "Suppose one of you wants to build a tower. Won't you first sit down and estimate the cost to see if you have enough money to complete it? For if you lay the foundation and are not able to finish it, everyone who sees it will ridicule you, saying, 'This person began to build and wasn't able to finish'" (Luke 14:28-30). In other words, Jesus was telling them to look at what following Him would cost them before they made the decision to follow. If we begin and then realize the cost of following is too high, our witness will do a disservice to Christ.

Walking with God through life can be an exhilarating ride, but the cost is high if you're doing it right. Knowing what I know now about how the peace I have on the days I'm in step with the Spirit, there's nothing I wouldn't give up for that. It's truly what God made us for.

I want to end by sharing a poem I wrote which describes God's heart in giving us the choice to love Him first and follow Him:

> You could force us all to worship and adore You.
> You could take each mind and make it do Your Will.
> You could blind each heart to everything but You, God,
> But there's a depth of love that's proven through Free Will.
>
> You could unveil our eyes to cease Your mystery.
> You could cast our every ache and pain to sea.
> You could shield our hearts from pain and our lives from death,
> But that wouldn't form us into who You hoped we'd be.
>
> So I'll learn to trust the Maker who makes majesty,
> A God that sees much more than I can see.
> I'll pledge my life to all His life's desires,
> But for now, my God, just come and sit with me.

I'm praying for us today. I'm praying we can release the white knuckled clutch-hold we sometimes have on the things of this world and choose a life whose surrender reflects our love and commitment to Him above all else.

Discussion Questions

1. What people, goals, or material things are you tempted to place higher than God in your life? Remember, they're higher than God if you give more thought to pleasing them or living for them than you do God (it's more common than you think!).

2. In what ways can this person, goal or material thing become shakable if they're put before God in your life? If it's a person, they are probably aware of their heightened significance to you. What kind of pressure do you think this puts on THEM to not fail you or to live up to everything you want them to be?

3. According to Lamentations 3:21-24, how is God's love described? And what benefits do we have because of His love?

4. What does 1 Peter 1:22 call us to do for one another? What does this say about what the intensity of our love for God should be? (Also read Mark 12:30-31 if needed)

5. Before reading the part of the devotional surrounding Luke 9:57-62, did you tend to think of Christianity as a more casual, tack-on-to-your-week kind of faith? If so, what influences in your life or in our culture molded this belief?

Lettering #6

A B C D E F G
H I J K L M N
O P Q R S T
U V W X Y Z

1 2 3 4 5 6
7 8 9 0 ♡

IT IS WELL
WITH my SOUL

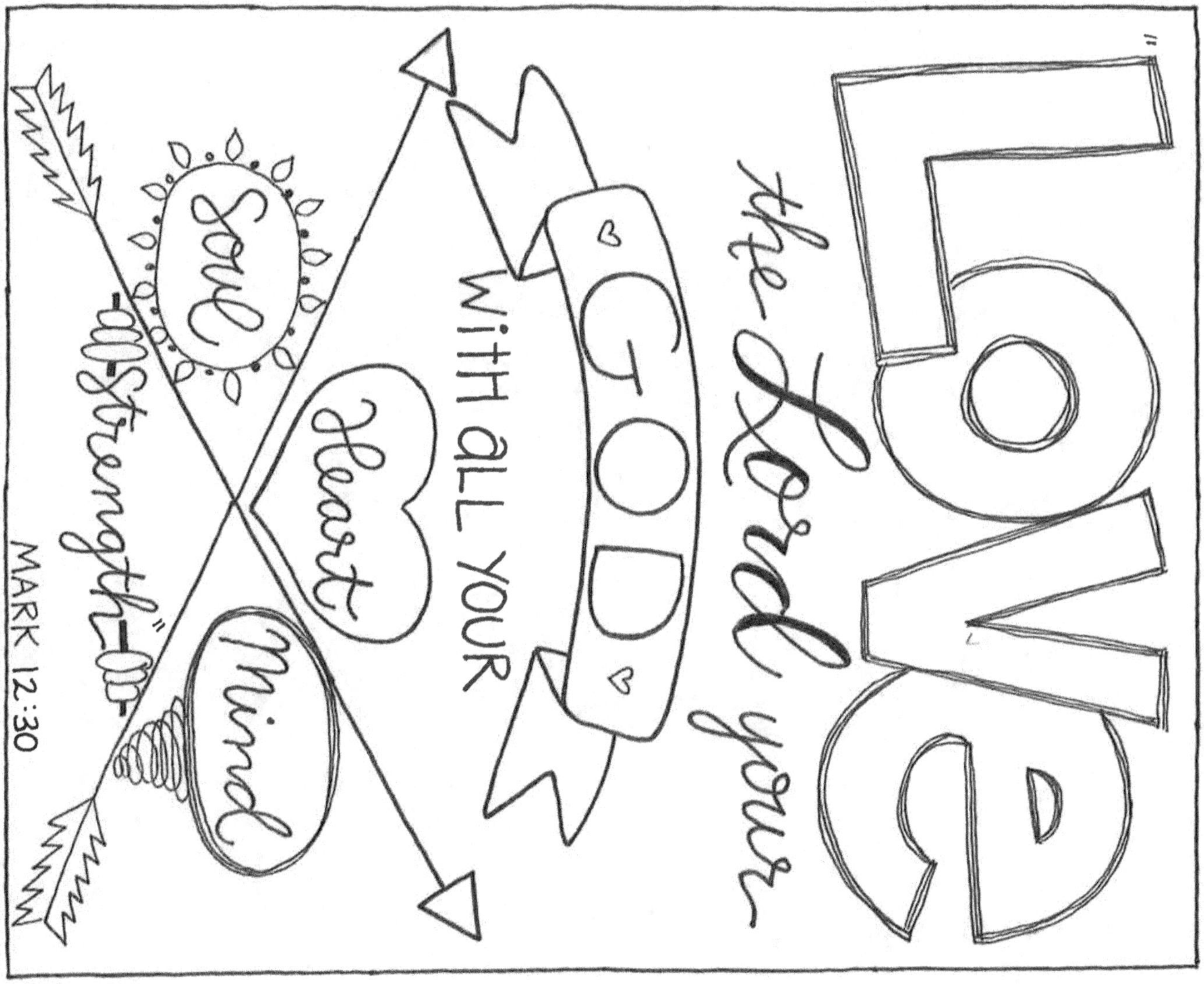

LOVE
the Lord your
GOD
with all your
Heart
Soul
Mind
"Strength"
MARK 12:30

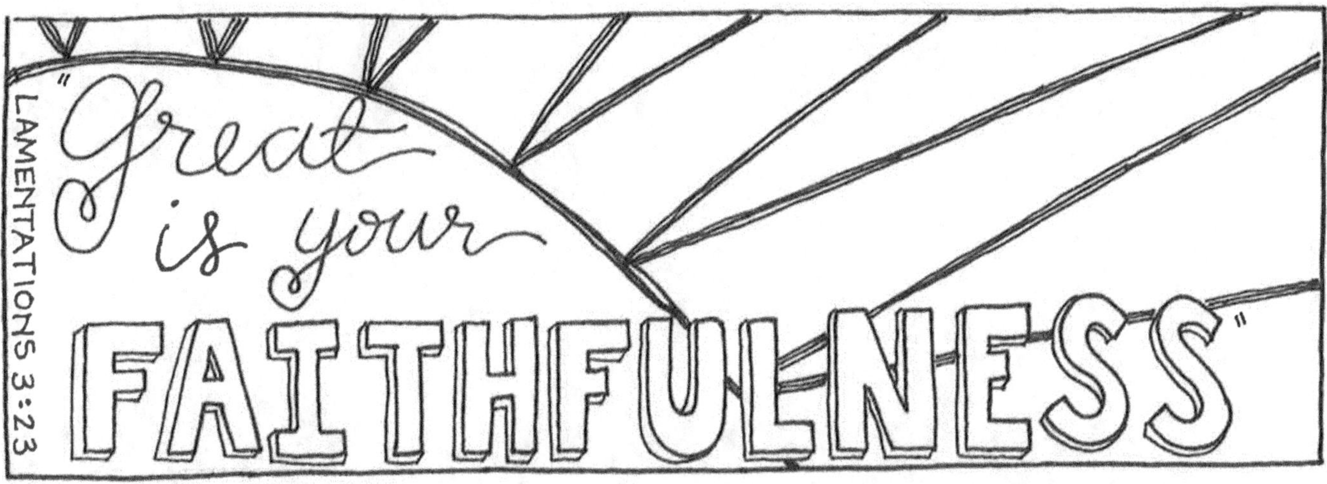

"Great
is your
FAITHFULNESS"
LAMENTATIONS 3:23

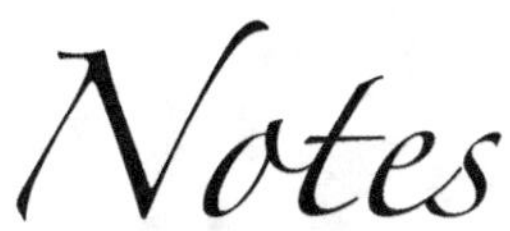Notes

Week One Devotional – To Be Kept
1. Beth Moore, *A Heart Like His: Seeking the Heart of God Through a Study of David* (Nashville, TN: LifeWay Press, 1996), 53.

Week Five Devotional – Abide in Me
1. Larry Crabb, *Real Church: Does It Exist? Can I Find It?* (Nashville, TN: Thomas Nelson, Inc., 2009), 42.